CARPENTER

COOL VOCATIONAL CAREERS

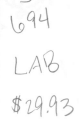

CHERRY
LAKE
Publishing

Published in the United States of America by Cherry Lake Publishing
Ann Arbor, Michigan
www.cherrylakepublishing.com

Content Adviser: Derek Macheske, Woods Construction Inc.
Reading Adviser: Marla Conn MS, Ed., Literacy specialist, Read-Ability, Inc.

Photo Credits: © Photographee.eu/Shutterstock, cover, 1, 20; © Minerva Studio/Shutterstock, 5;
© KristianSeptimiusKrogh/istock, 6; © goodluz/Shutterstock, 8; © elenaleonova/istock, 9 ; © Anita Colic/Shutterstock, 10;
© Urban Napflin/Shutterstock, 11; © inhauscreative/istock, 13; © sturti/istock, 14; © Tyler Olson/Shutterstock, 16;
© dotshock/Shutterstock, 19; © Susan Chiang/istock, 22; © Stuart Jenner/Shutterstock, 25;
© Blend Images/Shutterstock, 26; © Justin Horrocks/istock, 28

Library of Congress Cataloging-in-Publication Data
Names: Labrecque, Ellen, author.
Title: Carpenter / Ellen Labrecque.
Description: Ann Arbor : Cherry Lake Publishing, 2016. |
Series: Cool vocational careers | Audience: Grades 4 to 6. | Includes bibliographical
    references and index.
Identifiers: LCCN 2015049647| ISBN 9781634710596 (hardcover) |
    ISBN 9781634712576 (pbk.) | ISBN 9781634711586 (pdf) | ISBN 9781634713566 (ebook)
Subjects: LCSH: Carpenters—Juvenile literature. | Carpentry—Vocational guidance—Juvenile literature.
Classification: LCC TH5608.7 .L33 2016 | DDC 694/.023—dc23
LC record available at http://lccn.loc.gov/2015049647

Cherry Lake Publishing would like to acknowledge the work of the Partnership for 21st Century Learning.
Please visit www.p21.org for more information.

Printed in the United States of America
Corporate Graphics

ABOUT THE AUTHOR

Ellen Labrecque is a freelance writer living in Yardley, Pennsylvania. Previously, she was a senior editor at *Sports Illustrated Kids*. Ellen loves to travel and then learn about new places and people she can write about in her books.

TABLE OF CONTENTS

Getting Started

Jerry Smith sits down with a cup of coffee to look over his to-do list for the day. He has worked as a self-employed carpenter for the last 12 years. Today, he is working on redoing a customer's bathroom. He plans to lay **tile**.

"Each job is very different," Jerry explains. "This is why it is especially important for me to collect my thoughts every morning."

Jerry has to go to the hardware store to pick up some materials before he heads over to his job. He also has to make sure he has what he needs in his toolbox and tool belt.

After he picks up the supplies, Jerry arrives at the customer's home and spends some time talking with the homeowner. They carefully go over the work schedule together. They had already

4

Carpenters work with more than just wood.

Before a renovation, the carpenter gives the homeowner an estimate of the cost.

agreed on how much the **renovation** would cost. But they go over some of the pricing again. Jerry doesn't want the homeowner to be surprised by anything.

Jerry soon goes to work. At the end of the day, he carefully inspects the bathroom to make sure nothing was overlooked. Then he sweeps the floor and hauls away the old tile materials. The bathroom is starting to look brand new! Each day, Jerry tells the homeowner what will come next. Sometimes he might be ahead of schedule. Other times, he might be a little behind. He makes sure the owner knows exactly how far along the bathroom is.

People **remodel** bathrooms, kitchens, and other rooms for many different reasons. Sometimes water pipes leak and cause damage to walls or floors. Often, people just want to give an old room a new look. Carpenters can help them do all this and more.

Stores and restaurants also go through renovations sometimes. Some teams of carpenters specialize in these **commercial** buildings. Since these buildings are bigger, they usually take much longer to remodel than a house.

21st Century Content

According to the Construction Materials Recycling Association, construction waste is the largest source of trash in the United States. The association reports that 325 million tons of recoverable construction debris is generated in the United States each year. Materials such as wood, metal, and asphalt all end up in landfills. But more and more carpenters are starting to recycle their own material instead. They have learned new ways to reuse wood, steel, roofing materials, and even old windows!

Carpenters work both inside and outside.

Carpenters are skilled **construction** workers. They build, install, and repair structures made from wood and other materials. The structure may be a room or an entire home. That isn't all they do, though. Carpenters construct the buildings, bridges, and highways you see every day.

Many people think that carpenters work only with wood, but this isn't true. Ancient peoples built structures out of stone, brick, and mud. Today's carpenters work with these materials as well as metals, plastics, and concrete. They also use premade materials such as drywall, plywood, and hardwood flooring. During the

A sturdy house needs a strong foundation built by skilled carpenters.

Wooden ships needed to be strong enough to travel long distances.

Wheels were invented thousands of years ago.

Middle Ages, carpenters specialized in building things such as wooden ships, wheels, or barrels. They often lived in larger towns and traveled to smaller towns when needed. Before the 1800s, building materials were crafted by hand. Bricks, boards, and even nails were handmade. Then factories began **mass-producing** construction supplies and **prefabricated** materials. This put an end to the construction of completely handmade homes.

CHAPTER 2

What Carpenters Do

Stone Age people used stone axes to shape wood. They built animal traps, boats, and shelters. Egyptians used copper woodworking tools as early as 4000 BCE. By 2000 BCE, woodworking tools were made from bronze. Roman carpenters between 400 BCE and 500 CE used tools such as rasps, awls, and planes. Rasps look like files. They are used for shaping building material. Awls are like spikes. They can punch holes or mark wood. Planes are blades that make surfaces smooth. Many of these tools are still used today. Modern versions are made of different materials.

Today's carpenters do many different types of building. They build the wood frames for concrete **foundations**. They put up walls, build stairways, and hang windows. They install

As an apprentice, a future carpenter learns basic skills.

countertops and sinks. They even paint walls.

Carpenters start out as apprentices. Apprentices train with master carpenters for three to four years. If they pass the test at the end, they become journeymen. In time, journeymen become master carpenters.

Some carpenters, like Jerry, may work alone in a home. Others work as part of a team at a construction site. They may specialize in certain tasks. Rough carpenters are also called framers. They build the wooden framework for buildings. They also build concrete forms, **scaffolds**, and bridge supports. Finish

Safety goggles help protect a carpenter's eyes.

carpenters are also called trim carpenters. They install baseboards, doors, and windows. They also work with paneling, stairways, and trim. These are the things people will see when the building is complete.

Finish carpenters are more specialized carpenters. They do very detailed woodwork. They don't usually work on the construction of buildings. Most of their time is spent working at their shops making furniture and cabinetry.

Carpenters usually wear long pants, T-shirts, and work boots. They don't worry about getting their clothes dirty. Carpenters do worry about being safe. Sometimes carpenters work on people's roofs, and they have to be careful not to fall off of them. They also can encounter unexpected dangers in their work. Jerry once found a nest of copperhead snakes underneath a porch he was fixing!

Carpenters dress for safety. They wear boots with steel toes and heavy soles to protect their feet from sharp or heavy objects. They wear safety glasses or goggles to protect their eyes. Earplugs or earmuffs help protect their hearing. They often wear breathing masks if they are going to be around chemicals. Hard hats protect their heads at construction sites.

Life and Career Skills

What features would you want in a house you own someday? Maybe you want a place with tons of windows, or a huge staircase, or lots of space for a garden. Go online to research some of the most unique houses in the world, and write a paragraph about the kind of house you'd like to live in.

Simsbury Public Library Children's Room

Carpenters need to measure materials accurately.

Carpenters measure, cut, and piece together building materials. They use saws, drills, and many other tools. Rulers and squares help them measure materials. Plumb lines and levels help make sure materials are **aligned**. Stud finders tell carpenters where the wood supports are inside a wall. Ripping bars and crowbars help them pry materials apart. Glue, nails, and tape hold materials together. Wood pencils allow carpenters to mark their measurements on the materials. Chalk boxes are used to mark straight lines. Carpenters also use power tools such as sanders, table saws, and nail guns. These tools save time and help make work easier. Carpenters keep their tools in good working order. They may carry sharpening stones to keep their tools from getting dull.

Carpenters have one important tool that the Stone Age workers didn't—digital technology! Most carpenters use their smartphones at each job site. Phones can be useful for sending e-mail on the go, calculating measurements, and taking pictures of progress. Sometimes the **foreman** at each site will use a tablet, too. Many apps have been developed specifically to help carpenters work more efficiently.

Life and Career Skills

According to experts, the five tools carpenters can't live without are:
1. *Tool belts: The easier it is to access your tools, the better.*
2. *Hammers: Carpenters can't do much without a trusty hammer.*
3. *Tape measure: Carpenters want every line and angle to be accurate.*
4. *Levels: Carpenters want everything to be perfectly level, too.*
5. *Utility knife: A good knife has many different uses.*

CHAPTER 3

Becoming a Carpenter

Carpenters have to be in good physical shape. They spend a lot of time climbing, bending, and kneeling. They lift heavy materials and hold them in uncomfortable positions. They work with sharp tools and noisy machines. They may work high in the air while standing on narrow ledges. Sometimes they have to work outdoors in bad weather. They often work very long hours during the summer. Carpenters like working with their hands. They have to be willing to work indoors and outdoors. Knowing how to properly use machines and tools is a must. Carpenters can picture what a room is going to look like long before it is done. Do you think you have what it takes to be a carpenter?

To be a carpenter, you need a good education. Math skills are very important. Carpenters need to understand angles,

To be a carpenter, you need to be able to lift heavy materials.

A well-drawn blueprint can help a carpenter visualize a room.

dimensions, and fractions so they can measure building materials. They also have to estimate how much material they need for a job. They have to tell homeowners how long jobs will take and how much they will cost.

Future carpenters don't just study math in high school. They also take classes in English, physics, and **industrial arts**. This helps them begin learning how to follow directions on **blueprints** and design drawings. Trade schools and community colleges offer classes for students to learn carpentry skills. Future

21st Century Content

The United Brotherhood of Carpenters runs a program for high school students across the country called Career Connections. It introduces high school students to the craft and trade of carpentry. Besides learning skills, they also learn about the trade as a career choice.

"Carpentry is a viable alternative to college, and our goal with this program is to give schools across North America the tools to present that option to their students," says Carole O'Keefe, coordinator of the UBC program.

To learn more about this program, visit www.carpenters.org.

Carpenters need to be able to communicate well with the people who hired them.

carpenters should also learn technical writing and graphics programs. Classes in industrial safety are a good idea, too. Schools and employers offer apprenticeship programs. Future carpenters can join their local union to help them get started in this career. All these programs are a great way for future carpenters to get hands-on job experience.

A carpenter's job experience and where he or she lives can affect how much money he or she makes. Most carpenters make between $12.00 and $35.00 per hour. Experienced carpenters can make $75,000 or more a year. The amount of money carpenters make also depends on the demand for new construction. Sometimes, there might not be much work available. Other times, they can make extra money by working overtime. Some carpenters may go on to become contractors. Contractors run construction businesses. They hire people to help them with big jobs. Carpenters need to learn about different kinds of building materials. Each material is best used for different things. The same is true of tools. Carpenters also need to know how to repair and take care of their power tools.

Finally, carpenters need people skills. They have to convince homeowners that they are right for the job. Carpenters also work with other **subcontractors** such as plumbers and electricians. Carpenters with better training and more skills have an easier time finding work.

Joining Forces with Technology

There are close to a million carpenters working in the United States. This number is supposed to grow by 24 percent over the next 8 to 10 years. Most of these carpenters say they wouldn't be able to do their work without their cell phones! It helps them land new jobs and keep in touch with clients while on the job, in case they need to ask any questions or if they run into a problem.

"I use my iPhone almost as much as I use my miter saw," says Matthew Nicholas, a carpenter in Michigan.

Matthew works independently, but most carpenters work for contractors. They help build and repair buildings. Others work for stores, schools, and the government. About one-third of them have their own businesses.

New tools and materials have changed the way carpenters do

Many carpenters use their cell phones while working.

A building's design is usually finalized by an architect before the blueprints are given to a carpenter.

their jobs. For example, wall panels, roof assemblies, and stairs are not usually built on the job site. Instead, they are made in factories. Carpenters use machines to lift the prebuilt pieces into place. Most of a carpenter's tools today are cordless. This makes it easier for carpenters to work and maneuver in their job site without worrying about getting tangled up with cords.

Modern carpenters also use computer technology, although it's usually architects who make the creative decisions. Computer-aided design (CAD) software helps them create blueprints and models of the projects. These can easily be resized and rotated on the computer. When the designs finally reach the carpenters, all that's left to do is build.

Carpenters used to rely on string and tape measures to determine where property lines were when they were setting up foundations. Today, they rely on lasers and Global Positioning Systems (GPS) to do work. This has made their work faster and more accurate.

21st Century Content

Carpenters are needed, even at one of the coldest places on Earth! The United States Antarctic Program hires carpenters to replace doors and furniture, repair storm-damaged windows, and even venture out into the cold and snow to fix and maintain field huts for the scientists working there. The best part of being a carpenter there is getting to see seals, sea lions, and king penguins out the window. The hardest part is making sure you brought all the right tools with you. There is certainly no hardware store in Antarctica to buy something you forgot!

Some carpenters use their computers to help with accounting or design, or to learn new techniques.

When carpenters had to use heavy equipment, they relied on the operator to set equipment blades and buckets at the right angle to cut and dig holes. Laser- and GPS-equipped machines can now make these adjustments to the machine's settings.

Accounting software helps self-employed carpenters run their businesses. Other programs help them figure out costs for jobs. Many carpenters who work independently today have their own Web sites to advertise their services. This can help them get more jobs.

Carpenters are always learning new tips and teaching themselves new techniques. They take classes as well as watch videos on various Web sites.

Carpenters help shape communities as they grow and change. They help create our homes, businesses, and other buildings. They also help update the things we already have by rebuilding and remodeling them. Their hard work ensures that our buildings are sturdy and pleasing to look at, both inside and out. With a little hard work, you can become a carpenter. Then you can leave your mark on the places where we live, work, and spend our free time.

"I love knowing things that I built will be around a long time after I'm gone," says Jerry the carpenter. "It is a really satisfying feeling and a satisfying career."

Think About It

Carpenters usually work more when the economy is good in our country. This means that people are doing well and have more money to spend. Why do you think carpenters have more work during this time? Why do you think carpenters have less work when the economy isn't strong?

California is the U.S. state with the most carpenters, with 73,040. Why do you think this is the case? Does the good weather in California help with the carpentry business? Why or why not?

Just 1.7 percent of employed carpenters are women. Why do you think this is so? What are some ways to get more women to become carpenters? If you're a girl, would you want to become a carpenter? Why or why not?

For More Information

BOOKS

Cornille, Didier. *Who Built That? Skyscrapers: An Introduction to Skyscrapers and Their Architects*. New York: Princeton Architectural Press, 2014.

Dillon, Patrick. *The Story of Buildings: From the Pyramids to the Sydney Opera House and Beyond*. Somerville, MA: Candlewick Press, 2014.

McGuire, Kevin. *The All-New Woodworking for Kids*. New York: Lark Books, 2008.

WEB SITES

Bureau of Labor Statistics—Occupational Outlook Handbook: Carpenters
www.bls.gov/ooh/construction-and-extraction/carpenters.htm
Read about the training carpenters need, how much they earn, and other information about the profession.

National Building Museum—Families/Teens
www.nbm.org/families-kids/
Learn different stories about buildings, architecture, engineering, and design, and check out some cool activities to do with your family.

This Old House—Family Projects
www.thisoldhouse.com/toh/info/0,,20168465,00.html
Watch videos and see step-by-step pictures of simple projects such as "Building a Sandbox," "How to Build a Fort," "Building Stilts," and many more.

GLOSSARY

aligned (uh-LINED) in a straight line

blueprints (BLOO-prints) detailed plans for a structure

commercial (kuh-MUR_shuhl) of or having to do with buying and selling things

construction (kuhn-STRUHK-shuhn) the business of building permanent structures

dimensions (dih-MEN-shuhnz) the measurements of something in length, width, and often height or depth

foreman (FOR-muhn) someone who is in charge of a group of workers

foundations (foun-DAY-shuhnz) the supportive bottoms or bases of structures

industrial arts (in-DUHS-tree-uhl AHRTS) a class in which students learn to use tools and machines to build and repair things

mass-producing (mas pruh-DOOS-ing) making large amounts of identical things in a factory

prefabricated (pree-FAB-rih-kay-tid) made ahead of time

remodel (ree-MAH-duhl) rebuild or renovate

renovation (REN-uh-VAY-shuhn) the process of remodeling

scaffolds (SKAF-uhldz) frameworks put up to support workers while they are building, repairing, or painting something

subcontractors (suhb-KAHN-trakt-urz) companies that are paid to take on part of the main contractor's job

tile (TILE) a square made of stone, plastic, or baked clay, often used to make roods or to cover floors or walls

INDEX